Truths 10 *About*
AMERICA'S CHRISTIAN HERITAGE

SAM KASTENSMIDT

D. James Kennedy
MINISTRIES™
TRUTH IN Action®

Fort Lauderdale, Florida

TEN TRUTHS ABOUT AMERICA'S CHRISTIAN HERITAGE

By Sam Kastensmidt

Cover and Interior Design: Roark Creative, www.roarkcreative.com

Published by D. James Kennedy Ministries

Printed in the United States of America

D. James Kennedy MINISTRIES™

TRUTH IN Action®

P.O. Box 7009
Albert Lea, MN 56007
1-800-988-7884
www.truthinaction.org
letters@truthinaction.org

Contents

Contents

Truths 10 *About* America's Christian Heritage

Introduction

To Understand Our Future, We Must Understand Our Past

While everyone may be entitled to his own opinions, no one is entitled to make up his own facts.

In recent decades, a new debate has emerged over the nature of America's heritage. It is being argued in the courts, the classrooms, and even on cable TV. Most Americans still believe that our nation owes its existence and its prosperity to our Founders' allegiance to Christianity and its teachings. However, a chorus of voices now argues that America was conceived as a secular nation. Ignoring the abundance of evidence to the contrary, this chorus insists that our nation was founded with the aim of creating a secular state—divorced from the Christian faith.

Which side is correct? Which side stands with the facts?

Regardless of which side you are on, it cannot be denied that America stands alone as the world's longest enduring constitutional republic. This is not by accident nor by chance. America has endured, thanks to the genius of our Founders and the unmerited blessings of Almighty God. If we are to preserve America's liberty, we must understand the foundations of our republic, and we must ensure that these foundations are preserved for future generations, for they are not only eroding—they are under attack.

President Woodrow Wilson wisely warned:

> A nation which does not remember what it was yesterday, does not know what it is today, nor what it is trying to do. We are trying to do a futile thing if we do not know where we came from or what we have been about.... America was born a Christian nation. Amer-

> ica was born to exemplify that devotion to the elements of righteousness which are derived from the revelations of Holy Scripture.[1]

Woodrow Wilson
(American Vision)

These are words you will seldom hear today. "America was born a Christian nation. America was born to exemplify that devotion to the elements of righteousness which are derived from the revelations of Holy Scripture." It cannot be stated any more plainly, and it is the goal of *Ten Truths About America's Christian Heritage* to give clear, plain, and convincing evidence that America's foundations do rest solidly on the Christian faith.

Dr. D. James Kennedy once wrote:

Dr. D. James Kennedy

> All nations that have ever existed have been founded upon some theistic or antitheistic principle....If we know our history, we know that America was a nation founded upon Christ and His Word.[2]

Most Americans still agree. According to a 2007 nationwide survey conducted by the First Amendment Center, sixty-five percent of Americans believe that "the nation's founders intended the United States to be a Christian nation." That survey also discovered that fifty-five percent of Americans believe that "the U.S.

Constitution establishes a Christian nation."[3]

Sadly, proponents of a revised brand of history—a history that claims America was created as a thoroughly secularized nation—are given a disproportionate amount of attention by the so-called mainstream media. Consider the claims of some of the leading proponents of secularism.

> Many fanatics are working vigorously to turn America into a Christian nation.... America has never been a Christian nation.[4]
>
> —FREEDOM FROM RELIGION FOUNDATION

> Our Founders knew that mixing religion and government only caused civil strife, inequality and very often violence in pluralistic societies.[5]
>
> —AMERICANS UNITED FOR THE SEPARATION OF CHURCH AND STATE

> The Founding Fathers ... rarely practiced Christian orthodoxy.... They understood the dangers of religion.[6]
>
> —EARLY AMERICA REVIEW

Such phrases and slogans have no support in history. The following ten truths present the true picture—America's founding took root in the Christian faith, and Christian ideals and principles guided its development. But we're not asking you to take our word for it. Read this booklet. Consider the words and deeds of our forefathers, and draw your own conclusions as you read *Ten Truths About America's Christian Heritage.*

Truth 1

America Was Begun as a "Church Relocation Project"

Historical records show that this country's founding was deeply and inextricably rooted in the Christian faith.

Christopher Columbus attributed his discovery of the New World to the guidance of the Holy Spirit. In Columbus' own words:

> It was the Lord who put into my mind (I could feel His hand upon me) the fact that it would be possible to sail from here to the Indies. There is no question that the inspiration was from the Holy Spirit.... Our Lord Jesus Christ desired to perform a very obvious miracle in the voyage to the Indies, to confront me and the whole people of God.[7]

Some modern historians claim that Columbus embarked on his voyages only in pursuit of fame and wealth, but Columbus' own writings reveal something different. Writing in his *Book of Prophecies*, Columbus explained that his greatest motivation for sailing across the vast Atlantic Ocean was rooted in "the fact that the Gospel must still be preached to so many lands.... [T]his is what convinces me."[8]

Christopher Columbus
(American Vision)

When Queen Isabella described Columbus' expedition to the Pope, she explained that Columbus was attempting "to bear the light of Christ west to the heathen undiscovered lands."[9] Indeed, when Columbus first discovered an uncharted island, he did not name the island after himself or the Spanish monarch or the new land's potential wealth. Rather, Columbus named the island San Salvador, or "Holy Savior."[10]

Jamestown settlers, led by Rev. Stephen Hunt, erected a cross and claimed the land for Jesus Christ.
(Stephen Reid English, 1873-1948, The Landing at Cape Henry, April 1607, 1928, Chrysler Museum of Art, Norfolk Virginia)

Likewise, the first attempts to colonize the territory which is now the United States were expressly undertaken for the advancement of Christianity.

Jamestown Settlers Claimed Land for Christ

Consider the establishment of Jamestown, our nation's oldest settlement. Upon arriving in the New World, the first thing these pioneers did was to erect a cross on the beach and claim the land for Jesus Christ. Dr. Peter Lillback, president of

The Providence Forum, has explained, "It is most remarkable that when these British settlers came to this new place … they didn't put up a picture of the king. They put up an emblem of the King of Kings, the cross of Jesus Christ."[11]

The First Charter of Virginia stated that the purpose for establishing Jamestown involved the "propagating of [the] Christian religion to such people as yet live in darkness and miserable ignorance of the true knowledge and worship of God."[12] One of the most celebrated events in the life of the community was the baptism of Pocahontas (a friendly native Indian) into the Christian faith. The rotunda of the U.S. Capitol building still features a beautiful painting depicting that event.

Two groups that exerted the most influence upon the founding principles of American government were the Pilgrims and the Puritans—whose zeal for the Christian faith was exemplary.

Pilgrims Seek Freedom to Worship

King James I had refused to allow the Pilgrims to worship freely without the "trappings, traditions and organization of a central state church."[13] James vowed to "make them conform themselves [to the Church of England], or else I will harry them out of the land, or else do worse!"[14] So the Pilgrims fled to Holland for relief, but they did not find a happy home there. There were economic hardships, and the Pilgrims feared that their children would

King James I
(American Vision)

The Baptism of Pocahontas hangs in the rotunda of the U.S. Capitol.
(Architect of the Capitol)

lose their English identity. After ten years in the Netherlands, the group began to think of venturing to the New World. Like Columbus and the first settlers in Jamestown, they also had the great hope, as their governor, William Bradford, later wrote, "for the propagating and advancing the gospell of the kingdom of Christ in those remote parts of the world."[15] In 1617 they set their sites on settling in the colony of Virginia.

Dr. D. James Kennedy often stated that "America began as a church-relocation project."[16] Indeed, this was the stated reason for their migration. William Bradford, elected governor of the Plymouth Colony in 1621, explained that the Pilgrims chose to separate from the Church of England because they wanted to see the "churches of God revert to their ancient purity and recover their primitive order, liberty and beauty."[17]

In his book entitled *The History of Plymouth Plantation*, Governor Bradford wrote,

> They shook off this yoke of antichristian bondage, and as the Lord's free people, joined themselves by a covenant of the Lord into a church estate in the fellowship of the gospel, to walk in all His ways, made known unto them, according to their best endeavors, whatsoever it should cost them....[18]

The Mayflower Compact

During their long voyage to America, a storm providentially blew the Pilgrims off course, and their ship landed north of their original Virginia destination. Because this placed them outside of that colony's jurisdiction, the Pilgrims took a bold step and wrote their own covenant charter for self-government, the Mayflower Compact. This unprecedented document proclaimed:

William Bradford
(American Vision)

> In the name of God, Amen. We whose names are underwritten … Having undertaken, for the Glory of God and the advancement of the Christian Faith

> … do by these presents solemnly and mutually in the presence of God and one of another, Covenant and Combine ourselves together into a Civil Body Politic."

Shortly after settling in Plymouth, the Pilgrims planted another church in Salem, Massachusetts. William Brewster, one of the Pilgrim leaders, declared, "The church that had been brought over the ocean now saw another church, the first-born in America, holding the same faith in the same simplicity of *self-government under Christ alone* [emphasis added]."[19]

The Pilgrims' concept of "self-government under Christ alone" was radically different from anything the world had ever seen. Yet they viewed themselves, as Bradford wrote, "even as stepping-stones unto others for the performing of so great a work."[20]

The words etched into Governor Bradford's gravestone still challenge us to remember the heritage these brave men and women have passed down to us: "What our fathers with so much difficulty attained do not basely relinquish."[21]

"A City Upon a Hill"

Unlike the Pilgrims, the Puritans were not Separatists from the Church of England. Nonetheless, they traveled to America seeking freedom from the corruptions that existed within the Church of England. Reverend Francis Higginson, a famous Puritan minister, declared, "We do not go to New England as Separatists from the Church of England, though we cannot but separate from the corruptions of it; but we go to practice the positive part of church reformation, and propagate the Gospel in America!"[22]

As their name suggests, the "Puritans" sought to restore purity in the faith and practice of the Church of England. They knew that the world would be watching—looking for every opportunity to slander the name of Christ if their settlement in New England failed. The seriousness of their intent was expressed by John Winthrop, governor of the Massachusetts Bay Colony, who declared:

> For we must consider that we shall be as a City upon a Hill, the eyes of all people are upon us; so that if we shall deal falsely with our God in this work we have undertaken and so cause Him to withdraw his present help from us, we shall be made a story and a by-word through the world, we shall open the mouths of enemies to speak evil of the ways of God.[23]

John Winthrop
(American Vision)

The Puritans' influence on America's future government would be immeasurable. As we will see in the next chapter, because they saw that God is the source of both liberty and law, they were able to establish a civil society that was governed not by the whims of rulers or kings, but by law.

Truth 2

The Founders Recognized God as the Source of Liberty and Law

Few objective historians would dispute that America's system of law and liberty is deeply rooted in the principles of the Bible and the biblical traditions of the Puritans.

Peter Marshall, former chaplain to the United States Senate, and an expert on America's spiritual heritage, declared, "The Constitution of the United States has a path of descent that you can trace directly back to Puritan New England."[24] Upon arriving in America, the Puritans quickly established a social order governed by law. In 1639, they adopted the Fundamental Orders of Connecticut, which served as the first governing constitution among the colonies. Connecticut still bears the nickname: the "Constitution State."[25]

The Puritans believed that the Scriptures offered "a perfect rule for the direction and government of all men...."
(American Vision)

Puritans Framed First Colonial Constitution

The Founders marveled at the genius of the Puritans' form of government. George Washington thought Connecticut's Constitution was so brilliant that he ordered every delegate at the Constitutional Convention to have a copy.

The preamble of this Constitution declared, "[T]he Word of God requires that to maintain the peace and union of such a people there should be an orderly and decent Government established according to God…." Likewise, it stipulated that all governing officials were bound to rule according to established laws and where those were lacking, they should govern "according to the Rule of the Word of God."[26]

The Puritans adopted Article I of their new constitution by unanimous vote, affirming, "The Scriptures do hold forth a perfect rule for the direction and government of all men in all duties which they are to perform to God and men."[27]

According to the Connecticut Department of State, the constitution established by the Puritans "was never regarded by the colonists as the source of their government, but as a protection for and guaranty of the government."[28] This belief has been handed down to subsequent generations of Americans. President John F. Kennedy declared in his Inaugural Address, "The rights of man come not from the generosity of the state but from the hand of God."[29]

Puritans Looked to Higher Source for Rights

The Puritan concept of law placed liberty under the guidance of the God of Scripture. Our Founders repeatedly asserted that this philosophy *alone* could guard the sovereign rights of the citizenry from the whims of a tyrannical government. John Dickinson, a signer of the Constitution from Delaware, stated,

> Kings or parliaments could not give the rights essential to happiness….We claim them from a higher

> source—from the King of Kings, and Lord of all the Earth. They are not annexed to us by parchments and seals. They are created in us by the decrees of Providence, which establish the laws of our nature.[30]

The Declaration of Independence declares that all men "are endowed by their Creator with certain unalienable rights." America's Founding Fathers surely understood that liberty was the gift of God. Thomas Jefferson, who penned the Declaration, feared the day when skeptics and governing officials would attempt to usurp the role of God as the Author of Liberty. He wrote:

> God who gave us life gave us liberty. And can the liberties of a nation be thought secure when we have removed their only firm basis, a conviction in the minds of the people that these liberties are of the Gift of God? … Indeed, I tremble for my country when I reflect that God is just; that His justice cannot sleep forever.[31]

Thomas Jefferson
(American Vision)

Jefferson wisely saw that if Americans would ever deny that God is the source of our liberties, we would surely suffer the consequences.

This was a major concern of America's Founding Fathers, and they spoke vehemently against it. Alexander Hamilton, a signer of the U.S. Constitution and a co-author of the *Federalist Papers*, described humanistic legal systems as nothing more than "absurd and impious doctrine."[32]

God's Law Is Supreme

Alexander Hamilton and the other Founding Fathers often quoted the widely read eighteenth century legal commentator, William Blackstone, who wrote:

Alexander Hamilton
(American Vision)

> The law of nature … dictated by God, Himself, is, of course, superior in obligation to any other. It is binding over all the globe, in all countries, and at all times. No human laws are of any validity if contrary to this.[33]

Rufus King, a signer of the Constitution from Massachusetts, echoed these sentiments. "The law established by the Creator," he wrote, "… extends over the whole globe, is everywhere and at all times binding upon mankind." King claimed that it is "the law of God by which he makes his way known to man and is paramount to all human control."[34]

America's Founding Fathers acknowledged that God is the source of both law and liberty. Likewise, they understood that our nation's government must adhere to His immutable principles in order to prosper. George Washington, in his first Inaugural Address, stated:

> [T]he propitious smiles of Heaven can never be expected on a nation that disregards the eternal rules of order and right which Heaven itself has ordained.[35]

Skeptics claim that Christians are trying to force some draconian form of theocratic rule upon America. But Dr. Kennedy often asserted, "In no way am I advocating a theocracy. All I am advocating is a return, as much as possible, to the faith of our nation's Founders."[36]

It was the faith of our Founders that enabled them to imagine a nation governed by laws that would be superior to any other, because they were laws established by the Creator. The following chapter will show how our Founders' faith also inspired them with the zeal to be willing to sacrifice their personal safety and to give up personal fortune in order to establish America as a new independent nation governed under the laws of God and providing liberty to all its citizens.

George Washington's inauguration
(American Vision)

Truth 3

Christian Zeal Fueled the American Revolution

Just prior to the Revolutionary Period, from around 1730 to 1770, our nation saw a radical Christian revival known as the Great Awakening.

Benjamin Franklin recalled the effects of this massive spiritual resurgence in his autobiography:

> It was wonderful to see the change soon made in the manners of our inhabitants. From being thoughtless or indifferent about religion, it seemed as if all the world were growing religious, so that one could not walk through the town in an evening without hearing psalms sung in different families of every street.[37]

Benjamin Franklin
(NOAA Photo Gallery)

The case has been made that it was this dramatic stirring of spiritual vitality that gave rise to the colonists' zeal for political liberty. Historian Paul Johnson wrote in his book, *A History of the American People*, "The Great Awakening was … the proto-revolutionary event, the formative movement in American history, preceding the political drive for independence, and making it possible."[38]

President John Adams, who was contemporary to these events, explained as follows:

> The Revolution was effected before the War commenced. The Revolution was in the mind and hearts of the people; and [the] change in their religious sentiments of their duties and obligations.… This radical

change in the principles, opinions, sentiments, and affections of the people, was the real American Revolution.[39]

The fact that the Great Awakening made the Revolution possible has been affirmed by loyalists of the British Crown, our nation's Founders, and historians. Still, some secular historians claim that "religious influences and movements, including the Great Awakening, had no influence whatsoever on what the men of the Revolution did or thought."[40]

Patrick Henry called fellow patriots to action on March 23, 1775, in his famous "Give me liberty or give me death" speech.
(American Vision)

Resistance to Tyranny: A Christian Duty

In 1774, the Massachusetts Provincial Congress declared, "Resistance to tyranny becomes the Christian and social duty of each individual." The Congress also urged the residents of Massachusetts to "continue steadfast, and with a proper sense of your dependence on God, nobly defend those rights which heaven gave, and no man ought to take from us."[41]

Perhaps the most famous speech of the Revolutionary era was delivered at St. John's Church, when Patrick Henry galvanized the resolve of fellow patriots, proclaiming:

> Sir, we are not weak, if we make a proper use of the means which the God of nature hath placed in our power. Three millions of people, armed in the Holy cause of Liberty … are invincible by any force which our enemy can send against us.… Is life so dear, or peace so sweet, as to be purchased at the price of chains and slavery? Forbid it, Almighty God! I know not what course others may take; but as for me, give me liberty or give me death![42]

This "holy cause of liberty" led Edmund Burke, a member of the British Parliament, to warn that the Christian zeal of the Americans would never abide under tyrannical rule. Burke urged Parliament to avoid war, noting that the colonists could never be subdued. "The people are Protestants," he explained, "and of that kind which is the most adverse to all implicit submission of mind

Edmund Burke
(American Vision)

and opinion. This is a persuasion not only favorable to Liberty, but built upon it."[43]

During the British debates in Parliament, Sir Richard Sutton read a letter from a Crown-appointed governor in New England, which warned, "If you ask an American, who is his master? He will tell you he has none, nor any governor but Jesus Christ."[44]

This was a sentiment that resounded throughout the colonies. The various committees of correspondence often included a familiar rallying cry in their letters: "No King but King Jesus."[45]

Consequently, Britain's King George III and the British Parliament often claimed that the American Revolution was little more than "a Presbyterian rebellion."[46] Peter Oliver, a British loyalist from Massachusetts, blamed America's uprising on fiery preachers, whom he called "black-coated mobs."[47] Their sermons were so stirring that America's clergymen gained the nickname "the Black Regiment," because of their black ministerial robes.[48]

True Religion and Civil Liberty Inseparable

One of these ministers, Reverend John Witherspoon, the president of Princeton University, was selected to serve on more than one hundred committees of the Continental Congress. As a delegate from New Jersey, he urged the Congress to vote for independence. "Gentlemen, New Jersey is ready to vote for independence," he proclaimed. "The country is not only ripe for independence, but we are in danger of becoming rotten for the want of it...."[49]

When the opportunity came, Reverend Witherspoon proudly signed his name to the Declaration of Independence. Just weeks earlier, he had proclaimed:

John Witherspoon
(American Vision)

> It is in the man of piety and inward principle, that we may expect to find the uncorrupted patriot, the useful citizen, and the invincible soldier. God grant that in America true religion and civil liberty may be inseparable....[50]

Witherspoon's influence was substantial. Princeton University still boasts of its illustrious alumni who studied under Reverend John Witherspoon. The list includes President James Madison, Vice-President Aaron Burr, nine cabinet officers, twenty-one United States senators, thirty-nine members of the House of Representatives, three justices of the Supreme Court, twelve governors, and numerous delegates to the Constitutional Convention.[51]

Witherspoon was so successful in stirring the souls of America's patriots and fellow preachers that, upon hearing of "the shot heard around the world," Britain's Prime Minister declared to Parliament: "Cousin America has run off with a Presbyterian parson."[52]

"Conspicuous" Help From God

The religious fervor born of the Great Awakening ignited

the passions of Americans, who clearly understood that true liberty can only exist in a nation "under God." Thus, at the signing of the Declaration of Independence, Samuel Adams, labeled by his contemporaries as the "Father of the American Revolution,"[53] announced, "We have this day restored the Sovereign to Whom all men ought to be obedient. He reigns in heaven and from the rising to the setting of the sun, let His kingdom come."[54]

Historians would have to revise history to claim that America was founded by men who were seeking to separate the influence of the Christian religion from government. Of the 56 signers of the Declaration, at least 24 held seminary degrees.[55] Five days after the Declaration was adopted, the Continental Congress approved the use of public funds to hire military chaplains.[56] General George Washington then sent out a letter to the various regiments, which stated, "The General hopes and trusts, that every officer and man, will endeavour so to live, and act, as becomes a Christian Soldier, defending the dearest Rights and Liberties of his country."[57]

Acknowledging that God had helped them win their freedom, George Washington reflected in a letter to Brigadier-General Thomas Nelson,

> The hand of Providence has been so conspicuous in all this [the course of the war] that he must be worse than an infidel that lacks faith, and more wicked, that has not gratitude enough to acknowledge his obligations [to God].[58]

The Founders viewed the struggle for liberty as a Christian compulsion. By the grace of God, against all human odds, the colonists defeated the most powerful empire of the day. They expressed their gratitude to Him for their victory in the peace treaty with the British, which began with the words, "In the name of the most Holy and undivided Trinity...."[59]

At the celebration of the 45th anniversary of the Declaration of Independence, John Quincy Adams, sixth president of the United States, declared,

> The highest glory of the American Revolution was this; it connected in one indissoluble bond the principles of civil government with the principles of Christianity.[60]

John Quincy Adams
(American Vision)

In the following chapter we will see how this "indissoluble bond" was forged in our constitutional government.

Truth 4

"Our Constitution Was Made Only for a Moral and Religious People"

"We have no government armed with power capable of contending with human passions unbridled by morality and religion."

With these sober words, President John Adams warned that the U.S. Constitution will not be able to sustain our liberties if the American people abandon virtue and religion. Adams stated:

> Avarice, ambition, revenge, or gallantry, would break the strongest cords of our Constitution as a whale goes through a net. Our Constitution was made only for a moral and religious people. It is wholly inadequate to the government of any other. [61]

John Adams
(American Vision)

John Adams was not alone in his opinion. This view was widely held by our Founding Fathers.

William Paterson, a signer of the Constitution from New Jersey, was appointed by George Washington to serve on the U.S. Supreme Court. He, too, understood the importance of promoting religion among the citizenry. "Religion and morality are necessary to good government, good order, and good laws," he wrote, "for when the righteous are in authority, the people rejoice."[62]

Religion Needed for Liberty

The Founders understood that Christian morality was essential for both the preservation of liberty and the stability of law. They knew that if Americans ever abandoned the biblical standards of morality, there could be no fixed boundaries to maintain either liberty or law. Consequently, there would be no end to the possibilities of national evil. They saw that the future of the nation was dependent upon the vitality of religion and the exercise of biblical morality.

The Constitutional Convention
(American Vision)

By 1838 this view had so penetrated the American social consciousness that the New York State Legislature declared, "This is a Christian nation. Ninety-nine hundredths, if not a larger proportion, of our whole population, believe in the general doctrines of the Christian religion. Our Government depends ... on that virtue that has its foundation in the morality of the Christian religion."[63]

Sadly, our nation is in danger of exchanging liberty for licentiousness. Our Founders feared such a day. They knew that if religion's influence were ever suppressed, no system of laws could ever hold up to the societal strains that come with rampant immorality.

In his book, *Original Intent*, historian David Barton documents the alarming rise of destructive behavior that has followed the U.S. Supreme Court's decision to remove Bibles from public schools.[64] Indeed, since 1963, our nation has seen a sharp increase of violent crime, drug abuse, unwed teen mothers, sexually transmitted diseases, divorce, suicide, single-parent homes, abortion, homosexual relationships, and pornography. This is not accidental, nor should it surprise us. The Founders clearly saw that when we remove the influence of religion from society, all society suffers.

Exit God, Enter Tyrants

Apart from religion, the only way for society to maintain order is through expansion of government power. James McHenry, a signer of the U.S. Constitution, once explained that "public utility pleads most forcibly for the general distribution of the Holy Scriptures.... In vain, without the Bible, we increase penal laws and draw entrenchments around our institutions."[65]

Fearing this expansion of government's role in society,

Patrick Henry proclaimed, "It is when a people forget God, that tyrants forge their chains."[66] He clearly saw that weakened morals would affect the public conscience, and then freedom could not be sustained.

Abraham Baldwin, a signer of the U.S. Constitution, also authored the Charter for the College of Georgia. In this charter, he warned that free governments, without the aid of religion and morality, would be plagued by "evils more horrid than the wild, uncultivated state of nature." He concluded, "It should therefore be among the first objects of those who wish well to the national prosperity to encourage and support the principles of religion and morality...."[67]

Most of our nation's Founders viewed the loss of public virtue as the greatest of all possible threats to America's liberties. For example, Samuel Adams, a driving force of the Revolution, warned:

A general dissolution of principles and manners will more surely overthrow the liberties of America than the whole force of the common enemy. While the people are virtuous they cannot be subdued; but when they lose their virtue they will be ready to surrender their liberties to the first external or internal invader.[68]

Samuel Adams
(American Vision)

Today, secularist organizations are quick to dismiss the role of biblical morality in America. Instead, these organizations have branded unqualified "tolerance" as *the* pillar of modern morality. However, our society must be careful when dealing with notions of public virtue. In words that could have been spoken today, Theodore Roosevelt rightly warned over a century ago:

> There are those who believe that a new modernity demands a new morality. What they fail to consider is the harsh reality that there is no such thing as a new morality. There is only one morality. All else is immorality. There is only true Christian ethics over against which stands the whole of paganism....

Theodore Roosevelt
(Library of Congress)

Twin "Pillars of Human Happiness"

There is much at stake in our choice. If our forefathers were right, America cannot survive apart from the influence of religion and morality. They were not giving flippant suggestions or off-hand remarks. Their counsel was given out of an earnest concern for the future security of our republic.

In his famous Farewell Address, George Washington stated his views bluntly. He boldly challenged the patriotism of any person who would work to suppress religion and morality. Washington declared;

Of all the dispositions and habits which lead to political prosperity, religion and morality are indispensable supports. In vain would that man claim the tribute of patriotism, who should labor to subvert these great pillars of human happiness.[69]

Our nation was established with the pillars of religion and morality supporting the structure of law and liberty. If we choose to exchange these for the shifting sand of secularism, we will suffer the gradual disintegration of our law and the eventual loss of our liberty.

Our Founders knew that widespread religious conviction could not coexist alongside rampant immorality, and any attempts to satisfy both would lead to political chaos. They sought to promote the merits of religion in an attempt to suppress immorality. Today, secularists and atheists are seeking to do just the opposite. But government cannot be neutral in this matter. It must choose to encourage either immorality or religious conviction. If the former is unleashed, the latter will invariably be suppressed.

Our task is to return our Republic to the proven wisdom of our Founding Fathers; "Our Constitution was made only for a moral and religious people." We will see in the following chapter that the only sound foundation of true morality is the Bible.

Truth 5

Our Republic Rests Upon One Book, the Bible

The Bible is the most often cited source in Founding era political documents. President Andrew Jackson said in reference to the Bible: "That book, Sir, is the Rock upon which our republic rests."[70]

President Calvin Coolidge stated,

Calvin Coolidge
(Library of Congress)

> The foundations of our society and our government rest so much on the teachings of the Bible that it would be difficult to support them if faith in these teachings would cease to be practically universal in our country.[71]

In 1982, *Newsweek* magazine published an article, "How the Bible Made America," which concluded that "historians are discovering that the Bible, perhaps even more than the Constitution, is our founding document."[72]

Nevertheless, modern secularists claim that our nation's founding was completely divorced from religion. The ACLU contends, "The Founders did not see law as biblically-based.... Neither the Ten Commandments nor biblical law get mentioned anywhere in the debates and publications surrounding the founding documents."[73] Likewise, Americans United for the Separation of Church and State claims that "the U.S. Constitution is a wholly secular document...."[74] Books, such as *The Godless Constitution or The Myth of a Christian Nation*, are devoted to painting a secular view of our nation's founding.

Newsweek Cover, December 1982
(American Vision)

The Bible's Role in Founding America

Political philosophers Donald S. Lutz and Charles Hyneman set out to investigate the sources of our nation's Founding era political literature. After reviewing an estimated 15,000 written documents from the period between 1760 and 1805, professors Lutz and Hyneman determined that the Bible was, *by far*, the most cited source, comprising some 34 percent of all quotations. In fact, the Bible was cited four times as often as the next most commonly referenced source.[75]

As for the ACLU's claim that America's founding documents do not mention biblical law, this study showed that the book of the Bible most commonly cited was, in fact, the one that contains the majority of the laws given by God to Moses on

Mt. Sinai. "Deuteronomy is cited more than John Locke or anyone else," noted Professor Lutz.[76]

John Locke
(Engraving portrait by Kneller/Newscom)

Significantly, the next most commonly cited sources came from the political philosophers Baron Charles Montesquieu, Sir William Blackstone, and John Locke—each of whom encouraged the incorporation of biblical law into civil law.

- Montesquieu, in his classic 1748 treatise, *The Spirit of the Laws*, explained, "We owe to Christianity, in government, a certain political law."[77]

- Blackstone, in his *Commentaries on the Laws of England*, wrote, "Upon these two foundations, the law of nature and the law of revelation, depend all human laws."[78]

- Locke, in his *Second Treatise on Civil Government*, stated, "Laws … must be made according to the general Laws of Nature, and without contradiction to any positive Law of Scripture, otherwise they are ill made."[79]

Scripture-Saturated Thinking

As Dr. D. James Kennedy noted, "The Constitution is largely the product of Christian men with a biblical worldview."[80]

James McHenry, a Constitution signer from Maryland,

held such a high view of God's revelation in Scripture that he proclaimed, "The Holy Scriptures… can alone secure to society, order and peace, and to our courts of justice and constitutions of government, purity, stability, and usefulness."[81]

Their Scripture-saturated thinking led our Founders to follow biblical principles in the establishment of America's governmental form and structure. They feared the consolidation of too much power into the hands of any one man or entity, because they had a biblical view of man. They accepted and believed the words of the Prophet Jeremiah, who declared that "the heart is deceitful above all things, and desperately wicked…."[82]

James Madison
(American Vision)

James Madison saw the implications of this clearly, and in arguing for the ratification of the Constitution in the Federalist Papers, he stated, "It may be a reflection on human nature, that such devices should be necessary to control the abuses of government…. If men were angels, no government would be necessary."[83]

Madison proposed a "separation of powers," dividing the government into three separate branches—an idea that mirrored the three functions of governance ascribed to the Lord in Isaiah 33:22: "For the Lord is our Judge [judicial], the Lord is our lawgiver [legislative], the Lord is our king [executive]."[84]

God-Given, Not Government Granted

Although we associate the Declaration of Independence with the proclamation that all men are "endowed by their Creator with certain unalienable Rights," the next sentence of the Declaration explains that "to secure these rights, governments are instituted among men." Furthermore, it asserts that governments are instituted in order to *secure* the rights that flow—not from men or documents—but solely from our Creator. This idea is likewise woven into the Constitution.

The Preamble to the U.S. Constitution addresses this issue at the onset, explaining—in language similar to the Declaration—that the document was adopted to "secure the blessings of liberty." The framers of the Constitution recognized that neither they, nor the government they were establishing, could *create* the blessings of liberty. Rather, they wrote the Constitution in order to form a government that would acknowledge that its task is to *secure* those blessings, which come from a higher source—Almighty God.

The Constitution gave deference to America's Christian traditions. For example, in Article I, Section 7, when speaking of the legislative process, the Constitution specifies that the President has ten days to sign a bill into law, "Sundays excepted." Why does the Constitution exclude Sundays? The Founders wanted to ensure that the Christian Sabbath was honored by the nation's government. To this day, the Sabbath is observed by the various departments of government.

Our "Guiding Geniuses"

The evidence proves that our nation was founded with reverence for the principles of Scripture. Our presidents and political leaders have continued to recognize the importance of maintaining that reverence. President Franklin D. Roosevelt told Americans:

Franklin D. Roosevelt
(American Vision)

> We cannot read the history of our rise and development as a nation, without reckoning with the place the Bible has occupied in shaping the advances of the Republic.... [W]here we have been the truest and most consistent in obeying its precepts, we have attained the greatest measure of contentment and prosperity.[85]

While speaking with a reporter from *Time* magazine, former Chief Justice Earl Warren stated:

> I believe no one can read the history of our country... without realizing that the Good Book and the spirit of the Savior have from the beginning been our guiding geniuses.... I believe the entire Bill of Rights came into being because of the knowledge our forefathers had of the Bible and their belief in it.[86]

Dr. D. James Kennedy, author of *What If America Were A Christian Nation Again*, wrote, "Our nation was founded upon the principles of the Bible and a reliance upon Almighty

God."[87] Indeed, one would have to ignore a great deal of America's history to deny the central role the Scriptures had in our nation's founding. In the following chapter we will see the role the Christian religion had in the establishment of our state constitutions.

Truth 6

Every State Constitution Acknowledges God

The First Amendment begins by declaring, "Congress shall make no law respecting an establishment of religion, or prohibiting the free exercise thereof."

For secularists and atheists, this language bans any and all interaction between church and state—no matter how minor—lest it somehow establish religion. Symbols of faith, such as crèche scenes, or acknowledgement of God, such as graduation prayer or Ten Commandments monuments, are forbidden under this understanding of the First Amendment—one which federal courts have generally embraced.

Many Christians, however, are more concerned with the free exercise of religion, guaranteed in the First Amendment, than with the improbable idea that, for example, a Ten Commandments display on public property somehow establishes a religion. The Founders, they point out, drafted the First Amendment to prohibit the establishment of an official taxpayer-supported national church, like the Church of England, not to divorce government and religion.

The Founders were not afraid to devote tax monies for Christian ends. They used public funds to support Christian missionaries; they used government buildings for church services; they encouraged the use of the Bible in the classroom; and they instituted days of prayer and thanksgiving. Nevertheless, they did not want to impose a national denomination, as the King of England had imposed the Church of England upon the people of Great Britain.

The States Can Foster and Encourage Religion

Although the Founders did not want a national church,

they did leave open to the *individual states* the option of establishing government-endorsed churches. Thomas Jefferson claimed that the "power to prescribe any religious exercise … must then rest with the states."[88]

Joseph Story, appointed in 1811 by President James Madison to serve on the U.S. Supreme Court, wrote that it was the duty of government "to foster and encourage" the nation's religious beliefs. In his *Commentaries on the Constitution of the United States*, Justice Story explained, "The whole power over the subject of religion is left exclusively to the state governments, to be acted upon according to their justice and the state constitutions."[89]

It is the duty of government "to foster and encourage" the nation's religious beliefs.

Joseph Story
(American Vision)

A look at these state constitutions shows that they had a concern for this subject. In his sermon entitled "Church and State," Dr. D. James Kennedy noted, "Through all fifty state constitutions, without exception, there runs … [an] appeal and reference to God who is the Creator of our liberties and the preserver of our freedoms."[90]

Writing in 1864, historian Benjamin Franklin Morris noted, "An examination of the present Constitutions of the various states, now existing, will show that the Christian religion and its institutions are recognized as the religion of the Government and the nation."[91]

States Endorsed Christianity

While some believe that state endorsement of religion ceased with the ratification of the U.S. Constitution, a quick survey through American history shows this is not the case.

Long after the ratification of the U.S. Constitution and well into the nineteenth century, some states had mandated particular denominations to be their official state religions. Massachusetts and Connecticut, for example, had identified the Congregational Church as the state church. Most other states, however, opted to endorse Christianity as their state religion, rather than endorsing any particular church, sect, or denomination.

The South Carolina Constitution of 1778, which was still in effect at the time the U.S. Constitution was ratified, declared, "The Christian Protestant religion shall be deemed, and is hereby constituted and declared to be, the established religion of this State."

Until 1968, the New Hampshire Constitution endorsed *evangelical* Christianity. The constitution explained that "morality and piety, rightly grounded on evangelical principles, will give the best and greatest security to government." It declared, however, that "every denomination of Christians demeaning themselves quietly, and as good citizens of the state, shall be equally under the protection of the laws."[92] This proclamation remained in the state constitution for nearly 180 years after the ratification of the U.S. Constitution.[93]

In 1818, three decades after the ratification of the U.S. Constitution, Connecticut adopted a new state constitution declaring, "Each and every society or denomination of Christians in this state, shall have and enjoy the same and equal powers, rights, and privileges; and shall have power and authority to support and maintain the ministers or teachers of their respective denominations…."[94]

Connecticut's flag bears the state motto, "He Who Transplanted Still Sustains." The motto's origin may be traced to Psalm 80:8: "Thou hast brought a vine out of Egypt: thou hast cast out the heathen, and planted it" (KJV).

State Funding for Christian Education

In early America, such declarations were not controversial, because the citizenry universally acknowledged that they lived in a Christian nation. Some state constitutions empowered the government to fund Christian education and worship. Until 1833, the Massachusetts Constitution mandated its state legislature to "require the several towns … to make suitable provision, at their own expense, for the institution of the public worship of God and for the support and maintenance of public Protestant teachers of piety, religion, and morality."[95]

More than a century after the ratification of the U.S. Constitution, Delaware approved language in its state constitution proclaiming, "[I]t is the duty of all men frequently to assemble together for the public worship of Almighty God; and piety and morality, on which the prosperity of communities depends, are hereby promoted."[96]

These are not aberrations from an otherwise secular system of government. America's Founders believed that the Christian religion should receive encouragement from the states.

State Religious Tests and Oaths of Office

Even though the framers of the U.S. Constitution endorsed Article VI, declaring that "no religious test shall ever be required" for a person serving in the federal government, it was understood that the states would be free to impose religious qualifications for their own government positions. In fact, some signers of the U.S. Constitution played major roles in drafting provisions in their state constitutions that barred non-Christians from holding positions in government.

For example, George Read and Richard Bassett of Delaware helped to draft the Delaware Constitution of 1776. It required the following oath for all government officers:

> I, ________, do profess faith in God the Father, and in Jesus Christ His only Son, and the Holy Ghost, one God, blessed for evermore; and I do acknowledge the holy scriptures of the Old and New Testament to be given by divine inspiration.[97]

Nathaniel Gorham helped to author the Massachusetts Constitution of 1780. It also required an oath of office, which stated, "I, ______, do declare, that I believe the Christian religion, and have a firm persuasion of its truth."[98]

William Patterson
(Hulton Archive/Getty Images)

Likewise, William Paterson endorsed the New Jersey Constitution of 1776, which imposed standards for attaining public office that specified that "all persons, professing a belief in the faith of any Protestant sect … shall be capable of being elected into any office."[99]

Such "religious tests" continued at the state-level long after the U.S. Constitution was ratified. Several state constitutions, including the Tennessee Constitution of 1870, prohibited atheists from holding public office. Tennessee declared, "No person who denies the being of God, or a future state of rewards and punishments, shall hold any office in the civil department of this state."[100]

No amount of revisionist history can erase the obvious evidence contained in America's state constitutions. The Founders, along with the authors of the various state constitutions, openly encouraged religious convictions among their citizens. These men recognized Christianity as the religion of the nation and their state governments. And, education being a power "reserved to the States" by the 10th Amendment to the Constitution, they established their schools to further the Christian religion, as we will see in the following chapter.

Truth 7

America's Schools Were Established to Advance the Christian Faith

"In my view, the Christian religion is the most important and one of the first things in which all children, under a free government, ought to be instructed."[101]

So said Noah Webster, who has been called the "schoolmaster to America." He published the nation's first dictionary, *An American Dictionary of the English Language*,[102] and in the preface, Webster declared, "No truth is more evident to my mind than that the Christian religion must be the basis of any government intended to secure the rights and privileges of a free people."[103]

Noah Webster
(American Vision)

From its earliest establishment, education in America was sustained and supported by the Christian religion. In fact, gaining a proper understanding of the Bible was seen as the primary purpose of education. The first law governing education was passed in 1647 by the Massachusetts Bay Colony. Its purpose—to ensure that children would be able to read and write the Scriptures. The law, famously known as the "Old Deluder Satan Act," declared:

> It being one chief project of that old deluder, Satan, to keep men from the knowledge of the Scriptures … Every township … shall forthwith appoint one within their town to teach all such children as shall resort to him to write and read.[104]

Eight years later, the New Haven Code of 1655 imposed literacy requirements so that "all their children, and apprentices as they grow capable, may through God's blessing, attain at least so much, as to be able duly to read the Scriptures, and … to understand the main grounds and principles of Christian Religion necessary to salvation."[105]

Textbooks Encouraged Devotion to Jesus Christ

The most popular textbooks of the founding era demonstrate that Christianity was considered vital to the education of America's youth. *The New England Primer,* first published in 1690, remained America's most popular textbook for more than one hundred years—selling roughly five million copies in a time when America's population barely reached four million.[106] Lessons contained inside the *The Primer* were saturated with the Scriptures and encouraged devotion to Jesus Christ.[107]

The New England Primer
(American Vision)

McGuffey's Reader eventually replaced *The New England Primer* as the country's most popular textbook. First published in 1836, this book was filled with biblical principles and religious instruction. It ultimately sold more than 120 million copies and was officially recognized as a public school textbook in 37 states.[108]

In the foreword to his *Reader*, William McGuffey stated:

> The Christian religion is the religion of our country. From it are derived our prevalent notions of the character of God, the great moral governor of the universe. On its doctrines are founded the peculiarities of our free institutions.[109]

Christian Education Essential to Preserve Liberty

The Founders knew that Christian education is essential to the preservation of liberty. One year after the U.S. Constitution was ratified, Samuel Adams, the "Father of the American Revolution," explained how America could "establish the permanent foundations of freedom and happiness." He wrote,

> Let divines and philosophers, statesmen and patriots, unite their endeavors to renovate the age by impressing the minds of men with the importance of educating their little boys and girls, inculcating in the minds of youth the fear and love of the Deity.[110]

Even those considered to be the least religious among the Founders supported the use of the Bible in schools. While serving as president of the Washington, D.C., school board, Thomas Jefferson authored the District's first plan for public education. He did not propose a new curriculum filled with secular textbooks. Rather, he included both the Bible and the *Watts Hymnal* as the primary books for students.[111]

Benjamin Franklin once argued that schools should "afford frequent opportunities of showing the necessity of a public religion … and the excellency of the Christian religion above all others."[112]

This view was nearly universal. In a unanimous 1844 decision, the U.S. Supreme Court contended that educational institutions should incorporate the Bible into their curriculum:

> Why may not the Bible, and especially the New Testament, without note or comment, be read and taught as a divine revelation … its general precepts expounded, its evidences explained, and its glorious principles of morality inculcated? Where can the purest principles of morality be learned so clearly or so perfectly as from the New Testament?[113]

Harvard College *(American Vision)*

Harvard Started for Christian Purposes

From the smallest grammar school to the greatest university, knowledge of Jesus Christ was the ultimate objective of all education in early America. In his book, *What If Jesus Had Never Been Born*, Dr. D. James Kennedy explains, "Almost every one of the first 123 colleges and universities in the United States has Christian origins. They were started by Christians for Christian purposes."[114]

- *Harvard University*, founded in 1636, stated in its rules: "Let every student be plainly instructed and earnestly pressed to consider well the main end of life and studies to know God and Jesus Christ which is eternal life (John 17:3) and therefore to lay Christ in the bottom as the only foundation of all sound knowledge and learning."[115]

- *The College of William & Mary*, founded in 1693, proclaimed that it was founded so that "the Christian faith may be propagated … to the glory of God."[116]

- *Yale University*, founded in 1701, issued this charge to its students: "Above all, have an eye to the great end of all your studies, which is to obtain the clearest conceptions of Divine things and to lead you to a saving knowledge of God in his Son Jesus Christ."[117]

- *Princeton*, founded by Presbyterians in 1746, still declares on its crest, "*Dei sub numine viget*," (Latin: "Under God she flourishes"). Jonathan Dickinson, the first president of Princeton once declared, "Cursed be all that learning that is contrary to the Cross of Christ."[118]

- *Dartmouth College*, in its original 1769 charter, stated that it was founded "for the education and instruction of youths … in reading, writing, and all parts of learning which shall appear necessary and expedient for civilizing and Christianizing the children."[119]

Dartmouth College *(American Vision)*

Rush: Only Foundation Is in Religion

These beliefs did not suddenly change during or even after the Founding era. In 1787, Congress passed the Northwest Ordinance proclaiming, "Religion, morality, and knowledge—being necessary to good government and the happiness of mankind, schools, and the means of education—shall forever be encouraged."[120]

Gouverneur Morris, the most active member of the Constitutional Convention, once stated, "Religion is the only solid basis of good morals; therefore, education should teach the precepts of religion, and the duties of man towards God."[121]

Benjamin Rush, a signer of the Declaration of Independence who helped found five colleges, echoed these sentiments:

> The only foundation for a useful education in a republic is to be laid in religion. Without this there can be no virtue, and without virtue there can be no liberty, and liberty is the object and life of all republican governments.[122]

Benjamin Rush
(American Vision)

Truth 8

Foreign Nations Acknowledge Our Christian Roots and Heritage

While secularists and atheists in America may attempt to rewrite our history and deny our Christian heritage, they cannot erase from the record the observations of our Christian heritage that have been made by other nations and their leaders.

In the last century, the free world stood toe-to-toe against the threats of atheistic communist regimes. Stalin, Mao, and Pol Pot imposed their tyrannical governments on their peoples. When skeptics point to the sins of wayward Christianity, such as the Crusades and the Inquisition, they almost always ignore the fact that these atheistic communist regimes were responsible for the deaths of tens of millions. The twentieth century closed as the bloodiest in the history of the world.

At the opening of the Cold War, America was seen by its Allies as the antithesis of Communist Russia's oppressive despotism. The world saw the brilliance of America's liberties shining against the darkness of a repressive and brutal Soviet regime. Furthermore, America was not only free; it was Christian. The rest of the world began to see the connection. In an address to the American people, General Carlos P. Romulo, president of the United Nations General Assembly from 1949 to 1950, declared:

> Never forget, Americans, that yours is a spiritual country. Yes, I know you're a practical people. Like others, I've marveled at your factories, your skyscrapers, and your arsenals. But underlying everything else is the fact that America began as a God-loving, God-fearing, God-worshipping people.[123]

Likewise, the Honorable Charles Habib Malik, elected

president of the 13th Session of the United Nations General Assembly and Ambassador to the United Nations from Lebanon, stated in 1958:

> The good (in the United States) would never have come into being without the blessing and power of Jesus Christ....Whoever tries to conceive the American word without taking full account of the suffering and love and salvation of Christ is only dreaming. I know how embarrassing this matter is to politicians, bureaucrats, businessmen and cynics; but, whatever these honored men think, the irrefutable truth is that the soul of America is at its best and highest, Christian.[124]

Margaret Thatcher
(Arnie Sachs / CNP)

Margaret Thatcher, former Prime Minister of Great Britain and an essential ally during the Cold War, urged America to remain loyal to its biblical foundations. "If you accept freedom, you've got to have principles about the responsibility. You can't do this without a biblical foundation," she explained.

> Your Founding Fathers came over with that. They came over with the doctrines of the New Testament as well as the Old. They looked after one another, not only as a matter of necessity, but as a matter of duty to their God. There is no other country in the world which started that way.[125]

These comments from objective foreign observers of

America's Christian identity are not idiosyncratic. They have been the pattern throughout our nation's history.

Different Founding, Different Result

America's Founding was unique. In America's first years as a constitutional republic, France underwent its own revolution—a revolution influenced by the so-called Enlightenment era philosophies. Unlike America's revolution, this revolution sought to exalt men above God and to eliminate Christianity's influence from government.

Such a turn of the national character in France did not come as a surprise. Nearly four decades before the onset of the French Revolution, America's Founding Fathers witnessed the deterioration of morals plaguing an increasingly atheistic Europe. In an effort to lure prospective immigrants to America's shores, Benjamin Franklin wrote a pamphlet in 1754 aimed at Europe's Christian families.

> [B]ad examples to youth are more rare in America, which must be a comfortable consideration to parents. To this may be truly added, that serious religion, under its various denominations, is not only tolerated, but respected and practiced. Atheism is unknown there; Infidelity rare and secret; so that persons may live to a great age in that country without having their piety shocked by meeting with either an Atheist or an Infidel.[126]

Indeed, the atheistic philosophies feared by the Founders ultimately led France into one of the bloodiest and most shameful periods in its history. Starting in the year the U.S.

The bloody French Revolution instituted a program of de-Christianization.
(American Vision)

Constitution was ratified, 1789, the French Revolution brought a regime to power in France which instituted a program of de-Christianization, imposing death sentences on clergymen, closing churches, destroying religious monuments, and outlawing public worship and religious education. The Christian Gregorian calendar was replaced with the French Republican calendar, which imposed a 10-day week and eliminated the Sabbath. Perhaps the greatest display of this regime's arrogant hostility toward Christian religion came when the goddess "Reason" was enthroned inside Notre Dame Cathedral.

America's Founders were utterly appalled by France's attempt to impose state-sanctioned atheism. In the shadow of the French Revolution, George Washington delivered his Farewell Address in 1796. Pleading with future generations to avoid the disastrous consequences that inevitably accompany atheistic regimes, Washington warned, "[R]eason and experience both forbid us to expect that national morality can prevail in exclusion of religious principle."[127]

Likewise, in 1798, Alexander Hamilton condemned the "disgusting spectacle of the French Revolution." Hamilton wrote, "The attempt by the rulers of a nation to destroy all religious opinion, and to pervert a whole nation to atheism, is a phenomenon of profligacy [wickedness]."[128]

Three Frenchmen Agree

Just decades after France's atheistic revolution failed, French historian Alexis de Tocqueville visited America, traveling extensively and writing his observations in *Democracy in America*. As a Frenchman, De Tocqueville had a unique perspective on the relation between Christian religion and liberty in American life.

Alexis de Tocqueville
(American Vision)

> Upon my arrival in the United States the religious aspect of the country was the first thing that struck my attention.... In France I had almost always seen the spirit of religion and the spirit of freedom marching in opposite directions. But in America I found they were intimately united and that they reigned in common over the same country[129] ... The Americans combine the notions of Christianity and of liberty so intimately in their minds, that it is impossible to make them conceive the one without the other.[130]

The French revolutionary regime attempted to impose its atheistic ideology as a means to become an "enlightened" nation, but Tocqueville commented that the Christian faith—not atheistic secularism—had helped America become "the most enlightened and free nation of the earth."

In his book, *A Moral and Political Sketch of the United States*, French historian Achille Murat likewise stated,

> There is no country in which the people are so religious as in the United States; to the eyes of a foreigner they even appear to be too much so.... [But] while a death-struggle is waging in Europe... it is curious to observe the tranquility which prevails in the United States.[131]

Gustave de Beaumont, another French historian, wrote:

> Religion in America is not only a moral institution but also a political institution. All of the American constitutions exhort the citizens to practice religious worship as a safeguard both to good morals and to public liberties. In the United States, the law is never atheistic....[132]

Even the British feminist writer of the same time period, Harriet Martineau, conceded, "The institutions in America are, as I have said, planted down deep into Christianity." Though Martineau, a Unitarian, called the Christian faith a "monstrous superstition," she marveled at the success and prosperity of America, which she labeled "the most glorious temple of society that has ever yet been reared."[133]

Throughout America's history, foreign observers have recognized that America's successes have come because of its unique allegiance to the God of the Bible. Without that allegiance, America cannot expect to retain either the blessings of freedom or the prosperity that it now enjoys.

Truth 9

Presidents, Congresses, and Our Nation's Capitol Declare Our Belief in God

Without God there could be no American form of government, nor an American way of life. Recognition of the Supreme Being is the first—the most basic—expression of Americanism.

Dwight D. Eisenhower
(American Vision)

President Dwight D. Eisenhower stated it clearly—our American way of life is firmly rooted in our belief in God. He also noted, as we have shown in previous chapters, that this was the case from the very beginning of our nation; "Thus the founding fathers of America saw it, and thus with God's help, it will continue to be."[134]

Indeed, our nation's acknowledgement of its Christian roots did not end with the founding generation. More than two centuries have passed since the Declaration of Independence birthed American liberty, and our nation's elected officials—both presidents and congresses—continue to recognize our nation's reliance upon Almighty God.

Every president has been sworn into office with his hand on a Bible. Likewise, every president since George Washington has acknowledged our nation's dependence upon God in his inaugural address. George Washington declared, "No people can be bound to acknowledge and adore the Invisible Hand which conducts the affairs of men more than those of the United States."[135]

Abraham Lincoln delivered his First Inaugural Address days before the start of the Civil War. He spoke to a country

Abraham Lincoln
(American Vision)

facing irreconcilable differences, giving words of encouragement, "Intelligence, patriotism, Christianity, and a firm reliance on Him who has never yet forsaken this favored land are still competent to adjust in the best way all our present difficulty."[136]

In his memorable inaugural address, John F. Kennedy urged Americans, "Ask not what your country can do for you; ask what you can do for your country.... Let us go forth to lead the land we love, asking His blessing and His help, but knowing that here on earth God's work must truly be our own." [137]

Benjamin Harrison
(American Vision)

But Presidents have gone beyond just ceremonial gestures and words to demonstrate America's commitment to religious faith. On three separate occasions, President Thomas Jefferson extended an act of Congress designating lands to missionaries "for civilizing the Indians and promoting Christianity."[138] In 1890, President Benjamin Harrison granted lands to organizations "for the purpose of missionary or educational work..."[139] Most recently, in 2001, George W. Bush launched the Office of Faith-Based Initiatives.

Congress Affirmed America's Christian Roots

The Oath of Office for all members of Congress declares, "I, _____, do solemnly swear (or affirm) that I will support and defend the Constitution of the United States ... So help me God."[140]

Both the Senate and the House open sessions with prayer, and both institutions have had paid chaplains from the beginning who offer Christian prayers. For example, Dr. Peter Marshall, the chaplain for the Senate in the late 1940s, offered this prayer:

> May it be ever understood that our liberty is under God and can be found nowhere else.... We were born that way, as the only nation on earth that came into being "for the glory of God and the advancement of the Christian faith."[141]

The U.S. Congress has affirmed the fact that our country's spiritual roots are in the Christian faith. Not only did the U.S. Capitol Building and other government buildings serve as places of worship during early administrations,[142] but the House Judiciary Committee at one point declared its view that, "At the time of the adoption of the Constitution and the amendments, the universal sentiment was that Christianity should be encouraged.... It must be considered as the foundation on which the whole structure rests."[143] Shortly after, the House of Representatives passed a resolution declaring, "[T]he great vital and conservative element in our system is the belief of our people in the pure doctrines and divine truths of the gospel of Jesus Christ....[144]

We might note that these statements were made in 1854, a time of great division and disagreement over the issue of slavery. It is significant that during times of national trouble, our leaders have turned to Jesus Christ and the God of the Bible for comfort and strength.

In the midst of the Civil War, the U.S. Senate endorsed legislation stating:

> [E]ncouraged in this day of trouble by the assurance of His Word, to seek Him for succor according to His appointed way, through Jesus Christ, the Senate of the United States does hereby request the President of the United States, by his proclamation, to designate and set apart a day for national prayer and humiliation.[145]

One century later, in the midst of the Cold War, Congress voted to incorporate the phrase "under God" into the Pledge of Allegiance. Fearing the atheistic philosophies of communist Russia, both President Eisenhower and Congress approved adoption of the phrase. Also at this time, Congress acted by joint resolution to make *In God We Trust* the national motto of the United States, stipulating that it appear on all currency. "In these days when imperialistic and materialistic Communism seeks to attack and destroy freedom, it is proper," declared Congress, to "remind all of us of this self-evident truth" that "as long as this country trusts in God, it will prevail."[146]

President Ronald Reagan, whose diplomacy eventually ended the Cold War, stated it succinctly:

> America needs God more than God needs America. If we ever forget that we are "One Nation Under God," then we will be a Nation gone under.[147]

Ronald Reagon
(Library of Congress)

Inscribed on Walls and Painted on Ceilings

Proclamations and legislation have testified to our allegiance to the Christian faith and references to our belief in God are written on our coins and bills—and on the walls of our public buildings.

Both chambers of the House and Senate feature this inscription, "In God We Trust," on their walls. In the Capitol Rotunda there are eight large oil paintings—four of which have spiritual themes. Christian historian David Barton notes that the paintings capture "two prayer meetings, a Bible study, and a baptism."[148] One of the paintings depicts men planting a Cross in the shores of the Mississippi River.[149] The inside of the dome of the Capitol building features a fresco of "George Washington rising to the heavens in glory,"[150] and the U.S. Capitol Building houses a prayer room with the words of Psalm 16:1 inscribed on the wall: "Preserve me, O God: for in thee do I put my trust."

It will take more than aberrant court decisions or misguided historians to erase our Christian heritage; it would

Stained glass window in Congressional Prayer Room in the U.S. Capitol building.

literally require wrecking balls and sandblasters. Even Barry Lynn, who as president of Americans United for the Separation of Church and State claims that our Founders intended to create a secular state, admits, "Clearly, there are many religious references on buildings across Washington, D.C.…

They are part of the history of the country."[151]

Our nation's belief in God—expressed by Presidents and Congresses, inscribed on our coins and printed on our money, and proclaimed on the walls of our nation's capitol—cannot be erased or denied. It is the foundation upon which America rests.

The painting, "Embarkation of the Pilgrims," hangs in the rotunda of the U.S. Capitol building.
(Architect of the U.S. Capitol)

Truth 10

The Courts Have Declared We Are a Christian Nation

The Anti-Defamation League, a staunchly secularist organization, found in a nationwide survey that 64 percent of America's adults now believe that "religion is under attack" in our country.[152]

The following two decisions certainly support that view. Consider the decision by the U.S. Supreme Court in 1980, which concluded:

> If the posted copies of the Ten Commandments are to have any effect at all, it will be to induce the school children to read, meditate upon, perhaps to venerate and obey, the Commandments.... [This] is not a permissible state objective.[153]

Even more anti-Christian is the wording of the decision handed down in the 2002 case against Judge Roy Moore in

U.S. Supreme Court building

the U.S. District Court in Alabama. The district judge, Myron Thompson, wrote,

> The state may not acknowledge the sovereignty of the Judeo-Christian God and attribute to that God our religious freedom.[154]

The Founding Fathers would be utterly astonished by these statements. John Jay, our nation's first Supreme Court Chief Justice, declared, "The most effectual means of securing the continuance of our civil and religious liberties is always to remember with reverence and gratitude the Source from which they flow."[155] He is also known for saying that, "Providence has given to our people the choice of their rulers, and it is the duty, as well as the privilege and interest of our Christian nation, to select and prefer Christians for their rulers."[156]

John Jay
(American Vision)

"We Are a Christian People"

The modern move toward secularism is a relatively new trajectory for America's courts. For most of our history, the courts have affirmed our nation's Christian heritage. They did not even shy away from labeling America a "Christian nation." As the Supreme Court concluded in an 1892 decision, "We are a Christian people, and the morality of the country is deeply engrafted upon Christianity."[157] And again in 1931 in *U.S. v. McIntosh* the High Court stated,

> We are a Christian people, according to one another the equal right of religious freedom and acknowledge with reverence the duty of obedience to the will of God.[158]

America's early courts understood the genius of America's founding—professing that the rights and responsibilities of all Americans were received not from government, but from their Creator.

James Wilson, one of the six original Justices appointed by President George Washington to serve on the U.S. Supreme Court, surely understood the intentions of the nation's Founding Fathers. He was a signer of both the U.S. Constitution and the Declaration of Independence. In a lecture on law, Wilson declared:

> Human law must rest its authority, ultimately, upon the authority of that law, which is divine.... Far from being rivals or enemies, religion and law are twin sisters, friends, and mutual assistants. Indeed, these two sciences run into each other.[159]

For the early courts, it was inconceivable to imagine an America divorced from the influence of the Christian faith. As John Marshall, America's longest serving chief justice (1801-1835), once explained:

John Marshall
(American Vision)

> The American population is entirely Christian, and with us, Christianity and religion are identified. It would be strange, indeed, if with such a

> people, our institutions did not presuppose Christianity, and did not often refer to it, and express relations with it.[160]

This was the prevailing tone of jurisprudence for more than 150 years, as our nation's courts held firm to the Founders' beliefs in God and the Christian faith.

State Courts Acknowledged Our Christian Heritage

The same beliefs have also dominated the views of the states' courts. As early as 1799, the state courts were declaring that Christianity is the "established religion," and that within that religion all denominations have equal place. The Maryland Supreme Court decreed:

> By our form of government, the Christian religion is the established religion; and all sects and denominations of Christians are placed on the same equal footing and are equally entitled to protection in their religious liberty."[161]

Interestingly, Maryland was originally established as a haven for Roman Catholics coming to the New World, and for some time they predominated in holding political offices.

State supreme courts have also asserted that America's citizens follow the Christian moral code. In 1811, the New York Supreme Court upheld the conviction of a man for blaspheming the name of Christ, explaining that:

> Christianity in its enlarged sense, as a religion revealed and taught in the Bible, is part and parcel of the law of the land.... We are a Christian people and

> the morality of the country is deeply engrafted upon Christianity.[162]

Later, in 1861, the New York Supreme Court ruled that America is a Christian society.

> This fact is everywhere prominent in all our civil and political history, and has been, from the first, recognized and acted upon by the people, as well as by constitutional conventions, by legislatures and by courts of justice.[163]

The Pennsylvania Supreme Court investigated whether Christianity was incorporated into its state law in an 1824 case. The Court concluded affirmatively, stating:

> Christianity, general Christianity, is and always has been a part of the common law.... [It] is irrefragably proved that the laws and institutions of this state are built on the foundation of reverence for Christianity.[164]

Our Laws Rest on Christian Principles

One of the clearest acknowledgements of our country's Christian heritage by the U.S. Supreme Court came in the case of the *United States v. Church of the Holy Trinity* (1892), which was cited earlier in this chapter. The Court offered its unanimous conclusion after an exhaustive study of our nation's historical records:

> No purpose of action against religion can be imputed to any legislation, state or national, because this is a religious people. This is historically true. From the

> discovery of this continent to the present hour, there is a single voice making this affirmation.... These and many other matters which might be noticed, add a volume of unofficial declarations to the mass of organic utterances that this is a Christian nation. We are a Christian people, and the morality of the country is deeply engrafted upon Christianity.[165]

Earlier, in the case of *Vidal v. Girard's Executors* (1844) the U.S. Supreme Court had unanimously upheld the Pennsylvania Supreme Court's *Updegraph* decision, stating that "the laws and institutions of this state are built on the foundation of reverence for Christianity."[166]

In this same decision the High Court labeled America "a Christian country," stating that "Christianity...is not to be maliciously and openly reviled and blasphemed against, to the annoyance of believers or the injury of the public."[167]

The Supreme Court has not only acknowledged our Christian heritage, it has used principles of biblical law in drawing its conclusions. For example, in the late 1800s, when polygamy was spreading through the Western states, the U.S. Supreme Court argued, "Bigamy and polygamy are crimes by the laws of all civilized and Christian countries" (*Davis v. Beason*, 1889).[168]

This trend continued into the twentieth century as the Court issued strong statements affirming our allegiance to the God of the Bible in such cases as *United States v. McIntosh* (1931), which was cited earlier. As late as 1954, in the case of *Zorach v. Clauson*, the U.S. Supreme Court declared, "We are a religious people whose institutions presuppose a Supreme Being."[169]

> **"We are a religious people whose institutions presuppose a Supreme Being."**
>
> **Zorach v. Clauson, 1954**

In order to promote their secular view of America's history, secularists and atheists must deny history and the overarching harmony of thought that dominated the courts for America's first 150 years. If America is to preserve its liberty for future generations, our courts must not abandon the Christian foundation of our country nor the legal system that was built upon it.

Conclusion

Can We Reclaim and Restore Our Christian Heritage?

> Almost all the civil liberty now enjoyed in the world owes its origin to the principles of the Christian religion.... The religion which has introduced civil liberty is the religion of Christ and His apostles.... This is genuine Christianity, and to this we owe our free Constitutions of Government.[170]

No one in previous generations would have disputed statements such as the above from Noah Webster. The Christian religion was encouraged by government. There were "few persons" in America, as Justice Joseph Story wrote in 1833, "who would deliberately contend that it was unreasonable or unjust to foster and encourage the Christian religion...."[171]

Yet this is no longer the case. There are many who are trying to use any means possible to remove all references to our nation's Christian heritage from public notice.

The Duty to Tell the Truth

In contrast to Noah Webster's *History of the United States*, quoted above, history books now regularly omit the facts about our nation's Christian heritage and the Founding Fathers' religious beliefs.

In the 1980s, Dr. Paul Vitz, of New York University, looked at social studies textbooks to determine their accuracy and fairness. His conclusion—"The nature of the bias is clear. Religion ... [has] been reliably excluded from children's textbooks...."

Professor Vitz leveled an indictment against the writers and publishers of these textbooks, stating:

> Religion, especially Christianity, has played and continues to play a central role in our culture and history. To neglect to report this is simply to fail to carry out the major duty of any textbook writer, the duty to tell the truth.[172]

David Kupelian

And what of this "duty to tell the truth?" David Kupelian, best-selling author of *The Marketing of Evil*, says that we are passing down a "different America" to our children.

> Our nation's founding religion is being attacked as never before. The Constitution is being twisted out of all recognition; history is being rewritten; and Christian teachings and observances are being shut out and shut up.... We are bequeathing a different America to our children.[173]

"Let us not forget. . ."

This trend runs counter to all the hopes of previous generations. Early American statesman Daniel Webster encouraged Americans, saying:

> Let us not forget the religious character of our origin. Our fathers were brought hither by their high veneration for the Christian religion. They journeyed by its light, and labored in its hope. They sought to incorporate its principles with the elements of their society, and to diffuse its influence through all their

institutions, civil, political, or literary.[174]

Americans have forgotten this heritage. We have forgotten that the institutions of society that make us unique and powerful were built upon principles found in Christianity—not in any other religion; not in secular humanism. If America is to preserve its glorious heritage of liberty, then we must reclaim and restore the allegiance expressed to the Christian faith by every previous generation of Americans.

Daniel Webster
(Duke University Rare Book, Manuscript, and Special Collections Library)

In the final chapter of his book, *What if America Were a Christian Nation Again?*, Dr. D. James Kennedy quoted General Douglas MacArthur, who oversaw the rebuilding of Japan after World War II. What did MacArthur recommend for this shattered nation to help it remake itself after the war? Ten thousand missionaries. He rightly saw that with its defeat, Japan had lost all its moral and religious underpinnings. Its society would need a new religious founding to avoid moral decay. As MacArthur

General Douglas MacArthur, circa 1945, with Japanese Emperor Hirohito at the United States Embassy in Tokyo
(Keystone/Getty Images)

further observed:

> History fails to record a single precedent in which nations subject to moral decay have not passed into political and economic decline. There has been either a spiritual awakening to overcome the moral lapse, or a progressive deterioration leading to ultimate national disaster.[175]

Japan did not experience a new religious founding. If anything, its culture is clearly driven by materialism, and its moral decline is now becoming more evident.[176] But what of our culture? Since the 1960s our nation has seen steady moral decline in all segments of society. What will be the future of our nation? A spiritual awakening? Or progressive deterioration leading to national disaster?

Francis Schaeffer

In 1982, Dr. Francis Schaeffer spoke of the need for revival among America's Christians. He, too, pointed out that we have forgotten our Christian heritage. But he noted that true revival doesn't just bring about salvation of the lost and the fullness of the Holy Spirit in men and women's lives. True revival, said Dr. Schaeffer, brings about social change in a nation. "Every one of the great revivals had tremendous social implications," he stated.[177] Such was the revival, as we saw in chapter two, that fanned the flames of liberty to kindle the American Revolution. Such were the revivals that fueled the passion to end slavery in both Great Britain and the United States.

If Dr. Schaeffer thought America's Christians had lost sight of their spiritual heritage in 1982, what would he say today? The Founding Fathers had a high view of human life; they treasured the liberty that gave them the freedom to worship and freedom of speech and assembly. Some gave their lives and some died in poverty; but they counted their sacrifices worth the cost to secure the blessings of liberty for future generations of Americans.

Do we treasure our nation's Christian heritage? Do we value the heritage that has given us the blessings of freedom and liberty and prosperity unmatched by any country on earth? Are we willing to take action to ensure that heritage is not lost and to reclaim our nation for Christ?

At the conclusion of *What If America Were A Christian Nation Again?*, Dr. Kennedy offered the following prayer for America:

> Dear Father, make us salt as well as light. Help us to render unto Caesar and unto You, O God, those things which are respectively Yours. Use us, we pray, in our generation to help transform this nation and reclaim it, O Christ, for You, and in that glorious reclamation, the people will rejoice. In Jesus' name we pray. Amen.[178]

Dr. Kennedy began the work of transforming this nation and reclaiming it for Christ. But the work he began is far from done. Will you pray this prayer and then allow the Lord to use you to become salt and light to our nation? Will you work to see that the Christian heritage of America is not lost, but rather shines even brighter for future generations? Will you?

ENDNOTES

Introduction

1 William Federer, *America's God and Country: Encyclopedia of Quotations*, p. 697, Amerisearch, Inc., St. Louis, Missouri, 2000.

2 Dr. D. James Kennedy and Jerry Newcombe, *What If America Were A Christian Nation Again?*, Thomas Nelson, Inc., Nashville, Tenn., 2003, p. 4.

3 First Amendment Center, "State of the First Amendment 2007," September 11, 2007. http://www.firstamendmentcenter.org/pdf/SOFA2007results.pdf

4 "Is America A Christian Nation?" Freedom From Religion Foundation, Nontract No. 6, 2007.

5 "Founding Documents," Americans United for the Separation of Church and State, 2007. http://www.au.org/site/PageServer?pagename=resources_founding

6 Jim Walker, "Little-Known U.S. Document Signed by President Adams Proclaims America's Government Is Secular," *Early America Review*, Summer 1997. http://www.earlyamerica.com/review/summer97/secular.html

Truth 1: America Was Begun as a "Church Relocation Project"

7 William J. Federer, *America's God and Country*, Amerisearch, Inc., St. Louis, Mo., 1994, p. 113.

8 Federer, p. 115.

9 A letter from Queen Isabella to the Pope. Cecil Jane, trans. & ed., *The Voyages of Christopher Columbus*, London: Argonaut Press, 1930, p. 146.

10 Peter Marshall and David Manuel, *The Light and the Glory*, Old Tappan, N.J.: Fleming H. Revell Company, 1977, p. 41.

11 Peter Lillback, interviewed on *The Coral Ridge Hour*, "Jamestown," produced by Jerry Newcombe, June 14, 2007.

12 First Charter of Virginia, 1606, granted by King James I, Ebenezer Hazard, editor, *Historical Collections: Consisting of State Papers and Other Authentic Documents; Intended as Materials for an History of the United States of America*, Philadelphia: T. Dobson, 1792, Vol. I, pp. 50-51.

13 William Bradford, *The History of Plymouth Plantation 1608-1650*, Boston: Massachusetts Historical Society, 1856.

14 Robert Merrill Bartlett, *The Pilgrim Way*, Philadelphia: A Pilgrim Press Book, 1971, p. 54.

15 William Bradford, *The History of Plymouth Plantation 1608-1650.*

16 Dr. D. James Kennedy and Jerry Newcombe, *What If America Were a Christian Nation Again?*, Thomas Nelson, Inc., Nashville, Tenn., 2003, p. 20.

17 Peter Marshall and David Manuel, *The Light and the Glory*, Old Tappan, N.J.: Fleming H. Revell Company, 1977, p. 108.

18 William Bradford, *The History of Plymouth Plantation 1608-1650.*

19 Leonard Bacon, *The Genesis of the New England Church*, New York: Harper and Brothers, Publishers, 1874, p. 475.

20 William Bradford, *The History of Plymouth Plantation 1608-1650.*

21 Federer, p.67.

22 Peter Marshall and David Manuel, *The Light and the Glory*, Old Tappan, N.J.: Fleming H. Revell Company, 1977, p. 155.

23 John Winthrop, 1630, Stewart Mitchell, editor, *The Winthrop Papers*, 1623-1630, Boston: Massachusetts Historical Society, 1931, Vol. II, pp. 292-295.

Truth 2: The Founders Recognized God as the Source of Liberty and Law

24 "Crosses and Constitutions: Documenting America's Christian Heritage," *IMPACT* Newsletter, Coral Ridge Ministries, July 2005. http://www.coralridge.org/imp/impact07056.aspx

25 "About Connecticut: General Facts and Descriptions," The State of Connecticut, 2007. http://www.ct.gov/ctportal/cwp/view.asp?a=843&q=246434

26 "Historical Antecedents: The First Constitution of Connecticut," The Connecticut Department of State, 2007. http://www.sots.ct.gov/RegisterManual/SectionI/firstconst.htm

27 Article I, Fundamental Orders of Connecticut, 1639, in the articles of the Constitution of Connecticut drawn up in Quinipiack (New Haven), Connecticut.

28 "Historical Antecedents: The First Constitution of Connecticut," The Connecticut Department of State, 2007. http://www.sots.ct.gov/RegisterManual/SectionI/firstconst.htm

29 John Fitzgerald Kennedy, *Inaugural Addresses of the Presidents of the United States: From George Washington 1789 to Richard Milhous Nixon 1969*, delivered on January 20, 1961, Washington, D.C.: United States Government Printing Office; 91st Congress, 1st Session, House Document 91-142, 1969, pp. 267-270.

30 David Barton, *Original Intent*, WallBuilders, Aledo, Tex., 2000, p. 87.

31 *The Writings of Thomas Jefferson,* 20 vols., Washington, D.C.: The Thomas Jefferson Memorial Association, 1903-1904, Vol. IX, Vol. II, p. 227.

32 Alexander Hamilton, *The Works of Alexander Hamilton*, Vol. II, edited by John C. Hamilton, New York: Charles S. Francis & Company, 1851, Vol. II, p. 43.

33 Ibid.

34 David Barton, *Original Intent*, WallBuilders, Aledo, Tex.; 2000, p. 337.

35 George Washington in his First Inaugural Address, April 30, 1789. Jared Sparks, ed., *The Writings of George Washington*, 12 vols, Boston: American Stationer's Company, 1837, NY: F. Andrew's, 1834-1847, Vol. XII, pp. 2-5.

36 Dr. D. James Kennedy and Jerry Newcombe, *What If America Were A Christian Nation Again?* Thomas Nelson, Inc., Nashville, Tenn., 2003, pp. 4-5.

Truth 3: Christian Zeal Fueled the American Revolution

37 Benjamin Franklin, *The Autobiography of Benjamin Franklin*, March 1791, Ch. 10, p. 192.

38 Paul Johnson, *A History of the American People*, New York: Harper Collins Publishers, 1997, p. 116.

39 Jedidiah Morse, *Annals of the American Revolution*, 1824, p. 217.

40 Hannah Arendt, *On Revolution*, New York: The Viking Press, 1963, p. 309.

41 George Bancroft, *Bancroft's History of the United States*, 10 vols., Boston: Charles C. Little & James Brown, 1838, Vol. VII, p. 229.

42 Patrick Henry, March 23, 1775, in The Second Virginia Convention given at St. John's Church in Richmond, Virginia. *The Annals of America*, 20 vols., Chicago: Encyclopedia Britannica, 1968, Vol. 2, pp. 322-333.

43 Edmund Burke, March 22, 1775, in an address to Parliament entitled "Second Speech on the Conciliation with America: The Thirteen Resolutions." Sidney Carelton Newsom, ed., Burke's Speech on Conciliation with America, New York: The Macmillan Company, 1899, 1913, pp. 28-29.

44 George Lillie Craik and Charles MacFarlane, *Pictorial History of England During the Reign of George the Third*, London: Charles Knight & Company, 1828, p. 161.

45 William J. Federer, *America's God and Country: Encyclopedia of Quotations*, FAME Publishing, Coppell, Tex., 1994, p. 59.

46 Jack P. Greene and J.R. Pole, *A Companion to the American Revolution*, Blackwell Publishing, Malden,

Mass., 2000, p. 63.
47 Jon Butler, "Religion and the American Revolution," Yale University, October 17, 2003.
48 *The Cambridge History of American Literature*, edited by Sacvan Bercovitch, Cambridge University Press, Cambridge, UK, 1994, p. 391.
49 Edward Frank Humphrey, *Nationalism and Religion*, Boston: Chipman Law Publishing Co., 1924, p. 85.
50 Varnum Lansing Collins, *President Witherspoon*, New York: Arno Press and *The New York Times*, 1969, I:197-98.
51 "Milestones: A Short History of Princeton University," *Princeton University Handbook*, June 2005. http://www.princeton.edu/hr/handbook/history.htm
52 Statement of D. James Kennedy, Ph.D., Testimony Before the Subcommittee on Oversight of the House Committee on Ways and Means," May 14, 2002. http://waysandmeans.house.gov/Legacy/oversite/107cong/5-14-02/5-14kenn.htm
53 William Vincent Wells, *The Life and Public Services of Samuel Adams*, Boston: Little, Brown, and Co., 1865, p. 375.
54 Samuel Adams, statement made while the Declaration of Independence was being signed. Charles E. Kistler, *This Nation Under God*, Boston: Richard G. Badger, The Gorham Press, 1924, p. 71.
55 David Barton, "God: Missing in Action from American History," WallBuilders, June 2005. http://www.wallbuilders.com/resources/search/detail.php?ResourceID=121
56 Continental Congress, July 9, 1776; American Army Chaplaincy—A Brief History, prepared in the Office of the Chief of Chaplains: 1946, p. 6.
57 Jared Sparks, ed., *The Writings of George Washington* 12 vols. (Boston: American Stationer's Company, 1837; New York: F. Andrew's, 1834-1847), Vol. III, p. 456.
58 George Washington in a letter to Brigadier-General Thomas Nelson, August 20, 1778. Jared Sparks, ed., *The Writings of George Washington,* 12 vols., Boston: American Stationer's Company, 1837; New York: F. Andrew's, 1834-1847, Vol. VI, p. 36.
59 "The Paris Peace Treaty of 1783," University of Oklahoma Law School, 2006. http://www.law.ou.edu/ushistory/paris.shtml
60 John Quincy Adams on July 4, 1821. John Wingate Thornton, *The Pulpit of the American Revolution*, reprinted N.Y.: Burt Franklin, 1860; 1970, p. 29.

Truth 4: "Our Constitution Was Made Only for a Moral and Religious People"

61 President John Adams, October 11, 1798. Charles Francis Adams, ed., *The Works of John Adams*, Boston: Little, Brown, & Co., 1854, Vol. IX, pp. 228-229.
62 William Paterson, May 24, 1800. Maeva Marcus, editor, *The Documentary History of the Supreme Court of the United States*, 1789-1800, New York: Columbia University Press, 1988, Vol. III, p. 436.
63 Benjamin Franklin Morris, *The Christian Life and Character of the Civil Institutions of the United States*, Philadelphia, Penn.: L. Johnson & Co., 1863, p. 238.
64 David Barton, *Original Intent*, WallBuilder Press, Aledo, Tex., 2000, pp. 242-246.
65 Bernard Steiner, *One Hundred and Ten Years of Bible Society in Maryland*, Maryland: Maryland Bible Society, 1921, p. 14.
66 Tryon Edwards, *The New Dictionary of Thoughts—A Cyclopedia of Quotations*, Garden City, N.Y.: Hanover House, 1852, p. 300.
67 Charles C. Jones, *Biographical Sketches of the Delegates from Georgia*, Tustin, Calif.: American Biography Service, pp. 6-7.
68 *The Writings of Samuel Adams*, Harry Alonzo Cushing, New York: G.P. Putnam's Sons, 1908, p. 124.

69 George Washington's Farewell Address, September 19, 1796. Jared Sparks, ed., *The Writings of George Washington* 12 vols., Boston: American Stationer's Company, 1837; New York: F. Andrew's, 1834-1847, Vol. XII, pp. 227-228.

Truth 5: Our Republic Rests Upon One Book, the Bible

70 Gary DeMar, *America's Christian History: The Untold Story*, Atlanta, Ga., American Vision Publishers, Inc., 1993, p. 59.

71 John Calvin Coolidge (1923), Charles Fadiman, ed., *The American Treasury*, N.Y.: Harper & Brothers, Publishers, 1955, p. 127.

72 "How the Bible Made America," *Newsweek*, December 27, 1982.

73 ACLU of Kentucky, Writ Of Certiorari To The United States Court Of Appeals For The Sixth Circuit, *McCreary County v. ACLU of Kentucky*, No. 03-1693. http://www.aclu.org/FilesPDFs/mcreary.pdf

74 "Is America 'A Christian Nation?'" Americans United for the Separation of Church and State, 2007. http://www.au.org/site/News2?abbr=resources&page=NewsArticle&id=9061&security=1441&news_iv_ctrl=2422

75 Donald S. Lutz and Charles S. Hyneman, "The Relative Influence of European Writers on Late Eighteenth-Century American Political Thought" (1760-1805), *American Political Science Review*, 189-197, 1984.

76 "Crosses and Constitutions: Documenting America's Christian Heritage," *IMPACT* Newsletter, Coral Ridge Ministries, July 2005. http://www.coralridge.org/imp/impact07056.aspx

77 John Locke, *The Second Treatise on Civil Government*, 1690, reprinted Buffalo, N.Y.: Prometheus Books, 1986, p. 76, n. 1.

78 John Eidsmoe, *Christianity and the Constitution—The Faith of Our Founding Fathers*, Grand Rapids, Mich: Baker Book House, A Mott Media Book, 1993, pp. 55-56.

79 Sir William Blackstone, *Commentaries on the Laws of England*, Philadelphia: J.B. Lippincott and Co., 1879, Vol. I, pp. 42.

80 Dr. D. James Kennedy, *One Nation Under God*, DVD, July 2005. Available from Coral Ridge Ministries. Visit www.coralridge.org or call 1-800-988-7884.

81 James McHenry/Bernard Steiner, *One Hundred and Ten Years of Bible Society in Maryland*, Maryland: Maryland Bible Society, 1921, p. 14.

82 Baron Charles Montesquieu, The Spirit of the Laws, 1748, Anne Cohler, trans., reprinted Cambridge: Cambridge University Press, 1989, p. 457.

83 James Madison, *The Federalist,* No. 51, "The Structure of the Government Must Furnish the Proper Checks and Balances Between the Different Departments," *Independent Journal*, February 6, 1788.

84 Charles W. Pickering, *Supreme Chaos: The Politics of Judicial Confirmation & the Culture War*, Macon, Ga.: Stroud & Hall Publishers, 2005, p. 50.

85 Gary DeMar, *America's Christian History: The Untold Story* (p. 60), American Vision Publishers, Inc., Atlanta, Ga., 1993.

86 Chief Justice Earl Warren, February 14, 1954, as Chief Justice of the U.S. Supreme Court, in an interview entitled "Breakfast at Washington," *Time* magazine, February 14, 1954, p. 49.

87 Dr. D. James Kennedy and Jerry Newcombe, *What If America Were A Christian Nation Again?* Thomas Nelson, Inc., Nashville, Tenn., 2003, p. 41.

Truth 6: Every State Constitution Acknowledges God

88 Thomas Jefferson, in a letter to Samuel Miller, January 23, 1808. *Jefferson Writings*, Merrill D. Peterson, ed., NY: Literary Classics of the United States, Inc., 1984, p. 1186.

89 Joseph Story, *Commentaries on the Constitution of the United States*, Boston: Hilliard, Gray, and Company, 1833, reprinted 1879, Vol. III, p. 731.

90 Dr. D. James Kennedy in his unabridged printed sermon entitled "Church and State." Tim LaHaye, *Faith of Our Founding Fathers*, Brentwood, Tenn. "Our nation was founded upon the principles of the Bible and a reliance upon Almighty God.": Wolgemuth & Hyatt, Publishers, Inc., 1987, p. 93.

91 Benjamin Franklin Morris, *Christian Life and Character of the Civil Institutions of the United States*, Philadelphia: George W. Childs, 1864, p. 237.

92 Francis Newton Thorpe, ed. *The Federal and State Constitutions, Colonial Charters, and Other Organic Laws of the States, Territories, and Colonies Now or Heretofore Forming the United States of America*. 7 vols. Washington, D.C.: Government Printing Office, 1909.

93 Susan E. Marshall, *The New Hampshire State Constitution: A Reference Guide*, Westport, Conn.: Praeger Publishers, 2004, p. 26.

94 Constitution of the State of Connecticut (1818), Article VII, Section 1. *The Constitutions of the Several States Composing the Union*, Philadelphia: Hogan and Thompson, 1838, p. 110.

95 William J. Henry and William Logan Harris, *Ecclesiastical Law and Rules of Evidence*, New York: Phillips & Hunt, 1883, p. 310.

96 Delaware State Constitution, Article I, Section 1.

97 1776 Constitution of Delaware, The Avalon Project at Yale Law School. http://www.yale.edu/lawweb/avalon/states/de02.htm#1

98 Constitution of the Commonwealth of Massachusetts, http://www.mass.gov/legis/const.htm

99 The New Jersey Constitution of 1776, Article XIX, http://www.state.nj.us/njfacts/njdoc10a.htm

100 The 1870 Constitution of the State of Tennessee, Article IX, Section 2. http://www.tngenweb.org/law/constitution1870.html

Truth 7: America's Schools Were Formed to Advance the Christian Faith

101 Noah Webster, *American Dictionary of the English Language*, 1828 (reprinted San Francisco: Foundation for American Christian Education, 1967), Preface, p. 12.

102 Adam Cohen, "According to Webster: One Man's Attempt to Define 'America,'" *The New York Times*, February 12, 2006. http://nytimes.com/2006/02/12/opinion/12sun3.html?ex=1297400400&en=48fd62e8bf2712ca&ei=5090

103 Webster, *American Dictionary of the English Language*, 1828, Preface, p. 12.

104 "The First New Hampshire Teacher: John Legat," Museum of New Hampshire History, 2004. http://nhhistory.org/edu/support/nhgrowingup/firstnhteacher.pdf

105 *The True-Blue Laws of Connecticut and New Haven*, Edited by J. Hammond Trumbull, 1876. http://www.quinnipiac.edu/other/abl/etext/trueblue/bluelaws.html

106 David Limbaugh, *Persecution: How Liberals Are Waging War Against Christianity*, Harper Collins, New York, 2004.

107 *The Literatures of Colonial America: An Anthology*, Edited by Susan Castillo and Ivy Schweitzer, Blackwell Publishers, Malden, Mass., 2001.

108 Randy McNutt, "Oxford Pays Tribute to 'McGuffey Reader' Writer," *The Cincinnati Enquirer*, September 21, 2000. http://www.enquirer.com/editions/2000/09/21/loc_oxford_pays_tribute.html

109 William J. Federer, *America's God and Country*, Amerisearch, Inc., St. Louis, Missouri, 1994.

110 Charles Francis Adams, ed., *The Works of John Adams*, Boston: Little, Brown & Co., 1854, Vol. VI, p. 414.

111 John W. Whitehead, *The Second American Revolution*, Elgin, Ill.; David C. Cook Publishing Co., 1982, p. 100. Quoting from J.O. Wilson, Public School of Washington (Washington, D.C.: Columbia Historical Society, 1897), Vol. 1, p. 5.

112 Benjamin Franklin, *The Papers of Benjamin Franklin*, Leonard W. Labaree (Ed.), Yale University Press, New Haven, volume III, p. 413, 1961; "Proposals Relating to the Education of Youth in Pennsylvania," 1749.

113 *Vidal v. Girard's Executors*, Supreme Court of the United States, 1844.

114 Dr. D. James Kennedy and Jerry Newcombe, *What If Jesus Had Never Been Born?*, Nashville: Thomas Nelson, Inc., 1994, p. 52.

115 Harvard University (1636). Old South Leaflets. Benjamin Pierce, A History of Harvard University, Cambridge, Mass.: Brown, Shattuck, and Company, 1833, Appendix, p. 5.

116 Original Charter of the College of William and Mary, College (1692), The Charter and Statutes of the College of William and Mary in Virginia, Williamsburg, Va.: William Parks, 1736, p. 3.

117 Yale College (1755), The Catalogue of the Library of Yale College in New Haven (New London: T. Green, 1743), prefatory remarks. The Catalogue of the Library of Yale College in New Haven (New Haven: James Parker, 1755), prefatory remarks.

118 Reverend Jonathan Dickinson, president of Princeton University (1746). Stephen K. McDowell and Mark A. Beliles, America's Providential History, Charlottesville, Va.: Providence Press, 1988, p. 93.

119 The Charter of Dartmouth College (1754), charter granted to the Reverend Eleazar Wheelock in New Hampshire, Dresden: Isaiah Thomas, 1779, pp. 1, 4.

120 The Northwest Ordinance, 1787. http://usinfo.state.gov/usa/infousa/facts/democrac/5.htm

121 Gouverneur Morris, "Notes of the Form for the King of France," Jared Sparks, ed., *The Life of Gouverneur Morris, with Selections from His Correspondence and Miscellaneous Papers*, 3 vols., Boston: Gray and Bowen, 1832, Vol. III, p. 483.

122 Benjamin Rush, "Of the Mode of Education Proper in a Republic," 1798. http://press-pubs.uchicago.edu/founders/documents/v1ch18s30.html

Truth 8: Presidents, Congresses, and Our Capitol All Acknowledge God

123 Carlos Pea Romulo, president of the United Nations General Assembly (1949-1950), *Proclaim Liberty*, Dallas, Tex: Word of Faith, p. 13.

124 Russ Walton, *Biblical Principles of Importance to Godly Christians*, pp. 21-23, Marlborough, N.H.; The Plymouth Rock Foundation, 1984.

125 Margaret Hilda Thatcher, February 5, 1996, in New York City, in an interview with Joseph A. Cannon, entitled "The Conservative Vision of Margaret Thatcher," published in Human Events, Potomac, Md.: Human Events Publishing, March 29, 1996, Vol. 52, No. 12, pp. 12-14.

126 Benjamin Franklin, "Information on Those Who Would Remove to America," pp. 22-23, London: 1754.

127 George Washington, September 19, 1796, in his Farewell Address. Jared Sparks, ed., *The Writings of George Washington* 12 vols., Boston: American Stationer's Company, 1837; N.Y.: 1834-1847, Vol. XII, pp. 227-228.

128 Alexander Hamilton in a letter written on April 7, 1798. *The Works of Alexander Hamilton*, edited by John C. Hamilton, Charles F. Francis & Company, New York, 1851, pp. 650-651.

129 Alexis de Tocqueville, *The Republic of the United States of America and Its Political Institutions*, Reviewed and Examined, Henry Reeves, trans., Garden City, N.Y.: A.S. Barnes & Co., 1851, Vol. I, p. 337.

130 de Tocqueville, p. 335.

131 Achille Murat, *A Moral and Political Sketch of the United States*, London: Effingham Wilson, 1833, pp. 113, 142.

132 Gustave de Beaumont, Marie ou l'Esclavage aux E'tas-Unis, (Paris: 1835), Vol. II, p. 183ff. The Annals of America, 20 vols. (Chicago, Ill.: Encyclopedia Britannica, 1968), Vol. 6, p. 156.

133 Harriet Martineau, *Society in America*, New York, Saunders and Otley, 1837, Volume II, pp. 317-318, 366.

Truth 9: Presidents, Congresses, and Our Capitol All Acknowledge God

134 Dwight David Eisenhower, 1955, as quoted by President Gerald Rudolph Ford, Thursday, December 5, 1974, in a National Day of Prayer Proclamation.

135 George Washington in his First Inaugural Address, April 30, 1789. Jared Sparks, ed., *The Writings of George Washington*, Boston: American Stationer's Company, 1837, Vol. XII, pp. 2-5.

136 "First Inaugural Address of Abraham Lincoln, March 4, 1861," Avalon Project at Yale Law School, 1997.

137 "Inaugural Address of John F. Kennedy, January 20, 1961," Avalon Project at Yale Law School, 1997.

138 Daniel L. Driesbach, *Real Threat and Mere Shadow: Religious Liberty and the First Amendment*, Westchester, Ill.: Crossway Books, 1987, p. 127.

139 James D. Richardson, ed: *A Compilation of the Messages and Papers of the Presidents 1789-1897*, Washington, D.C.: Bureau of National Literature and Art, 1910, Vol. IX, pp. 95-96.

140 The Oath of Office for both the U.S. Senators and the U.S. Representatives: September 17, 1787; Donald A. Ritchie, *The Young Oxford Companion to the Congress of the United States*, p. 137, New York: Oxford University Press, 1993).

141 Catherine Marshall, ed., *The Prayers of Peter Marshall*, N.Y.: McGraw Hill Book Company, Inc., 1949, p. 186.

142 President John Quincy Adams wrote, "Religious service is usually performed on Sundays at the Treasury office and at the Capitol. I went both forenoon and afternoon to the Treasury." John Quincy Adams, ed. Charles Francis Adams, *Memoirs of John Quincy Adams: Comprising Portions of His Diary from 1795 to 1848*, Philadelphia, J.B. Lippencott & Co., 1874, p. 265.

143 United States Congress. March 27, 1854, Mr. Meacham giving report of the House Committee on the Judiciary. Reports of Committees of the House of Representatives Made During the First Session of the Thirty-Third Congress, Washington: A.O.P. Nicholson, 1854, pp. 1, 6, 8-9.

144 Resolution passed in the House of Representatives, May of 1854. Benjamin Franklin Morris, *The Christian Life and Character of the Civil Institutions of the United States*, Philadelphia: George W. Childs, 1864, pp. 327-328.

145 Benjamin Franklin Morris, *The Christian Life and Character of the Civil Institutions of the United States*, Philadelphia, Pa.: L. Johnson & Co., 1863, p. 558.

146 *Congressional Record*, 1956, p. 13917. http://www.nonbeliever.org/images/CR102-13917.pdf

147 Jeremiah O'Leary, "Reagan Declares That Faith Has Key Role in Political Life," *The Washington Times*, August 24, 1984.

148 David Brody, "Washington D.C.: Remembering Our Christian Heritage," CBN News, July 4, 2003.

149 "Paintings in the Capitol Rotunda," Architect of the Capitol, January 4, 2008.

150 "George Washington Rising to the Heavens," The Architect of the Capitol, January 4, 2008. http://www.aoc.gov/cc/art/rotunda/apotheosis/Overview.cfm

151 "Religious References Pervade D.C.," Fox News, January 26, 2005. http://www.foxnews.com/story/0,2933,145422,00.html

Truth 10: The Courts Have Declared We Are a Christian Nation

152 "Poll: Americans Believe Religion Is 'Under Attack'—Majority Says Religion is 'Losing Influence' In American Life," Anti-Defamation League Press Release, November 21, 2005.

http://www.adl.org/PresRele/RelChStSep_90/4830_90.htm

153 *Stone v. Graham*, 449 U.S. 39, Supreme Court of the United States, November 17, 1980.

154 *Glassroth v. Moore*, No. 01-T-1268-N, U.S. District Court for Middle Alabama, November 18, 2002.

155 William Jay, *Life of John Jay, with Selections from His Correspondence*, 2 vols., N.Y.: Harper, 1833, Vol. I, p. 457-58.

156 Supreme Court Chief Justice John Jay, statement made on October 12, 1816, *The Correspondence and Public Papers of John Jay*, edited by Henry P. Johnston, New York: G.P Putnam & Sons, 1893.

157 *U.S. v. Church of the Holy Trinity,* 143 U.S. 457, Supreme Court of the United States, 1892.

158 *U.S. v. McIntosh,* Supreme Court of the United States, 1931.

159 James Wilson, in his Lectures on Law delivered at the College of Philadelphia. James DeWitt Andres, *Works of Wilson*, 1:91-93, Chicago, 1896.

160 Daniel L. Dreisbach, Religion and Politics in the Early Republic: Jasper Adams and the Church-State Debate, University Press of Kentucky, Lexington, Ky., 1996, p. 113. Chief Justice John Marshall in a letter to Reverend Jasper Adams.

161 *Runkel v. Winemiller*, Maryland Supreme Court, 1803.

162 *People v. Ruggles*, New York Supreme Court, 1811.

163 *Lindenmuller v. The People*, 33 Barb. (NY) 548, The New York Supreme Court, 1861.

164 *Updegraph v. Commonwealth*, Pennsylvania Supreme Court, 1824.

165 *U.S. v. Church of the Holy Trinity*, 143 U.S. 457, Supreme Court of the United States, 1892.

166 *Updegraph v. Commonwealth*, Pennsylvania Supreme Court, 1824.

167 Decision of the Supreme Court of the United States in *Vidal v. Girard's Executors* (1844). *Life and Letters of Joseph Story*, editor: William Wetmore Story, Boston: Charles C. Little and James Brown Publishing, 1851, p. 463.

168 *Davis v. Beason*, 133 U.S. 333, Supreme Court of the United States, 1889.

169 Supreme Court of the United States, *Zorach v. Clauson*, 343 U.S. 306, April 28, 1952.

Conclusion

170 Noah Webster. 1832. *History of the United States,* New Haven: Durrie & Peck, 1832, pp. 273-274, 300, paragraph 578.

171 Joseph Story, *Commentaries on the Constitution of the United States*, ed: Melville M. Bigelow, Boston: Little, Brown, and Company, Cambridge University Press, Volume II, p. 629.

172 Paul C. Vitz, *Censorship: Evidence of Bias in our Children's Textbooks*, Ann Arbor, Mich.: Servant Books, 1986.

173 David Kupelian, *Whistleblower* magazine, "Criminalizing Christianity," December 2005. http://shop.wnd.com/store/item.asp?ITEM_ID=1789

174 Daniel Webster, *The Works of Daniel Webster*, Boston: Little, Brown and Company, 1853, Vol. I, p. 48.

175 Douglas MacArthur, May 12, 1962, speech to cadets at U.S. Military Academy at West Point.

176 In his 2002 book, *The New Japan: Debunking Seven Cultural Stereotypes*, (Yarmouth, Maine: Intercultural Press), social psychologist David Matsumoto claims that Japanese society is not so much characterized by "evil," but as showing an "absence of good," p. 124.

177 Francis Schaeffer, 1982, address to Coral Ridge Presbyterian Church, Fort Lauderdale, Fla. To obtain this message, request *Christian Manifesto*, from Coral Ridge Ministries. Available at www.coralridge.org or by calling 1-800-988-7884.

178 D. James Kennedy, *What If America Were A Christian Nation Again?,* Nashville, Tenn.: Thomas Nelson, Inc., 2003, p. 244.

Take the Next Step

You Have Read the Book. Now Watch the Video.

The ***10 Truths About America's Christian Heritage*** DVD offers a stirring look at the facts surrounding our nation's origin and infancy. Featuring experts with a commanding grasp of American history, The ***10 Truths About America's Christian Heritage*** DVD will take you even further in your understanding of America's Christian past.

Find More Resources to Inspire You

You can request the DVD, ***10 Truths About America's Christian Heritage***, by calling 1-800-98-TRUTH (1-800-988-7884). Or visit the D. James Kennedy Ministries webstore for this and many more unique resources that will inspire you, build your faith, and help you to put truth into action.

Visit our webstore at: **http://store.truthinaction.org.**